Scale

Scale

Nathan McClain

Four Way Books
Tribeca

Please direct all inquiries to:
Editorial Office
Four Way Books
POB 535, Village Station
New York, NY 10014
www.fourwaybooks.com

Library of Congress Cataloging-in-Publication Data

Names: McClain, Nathan, author.
Title: Scale / Nathan McClain.
Description: New York, NY : Four Way Books, 2017.
Identifiers: LCCN 2016034902 | ISBN 9781935536901 (pbk. : alk. paper)
Classification: LCC PS3613.C35724 A6 2017 | DDC 811/.6--dc23
LC record available at https://lccn.loc.gov/2016034902

This book is manufactured in the United States of America and printed on acid-free paper.

Four Way Books is a not-for-profit literary press. We are grateful for the assistance
we receive from individual donors, public arts agencies, and private foundations.

This publication is made possible with public funds from the National Endowment for the Arts

and from the New York State Council on the Arts, a state agency,

and from the Jerome Foundation.

We are a proud member of the Community of Literary Magazines and Presses.
Distributed by University Press of New England
One Court Street, Lebanon, NH 03766

Contents

III

for my daughter

The Fortress of Solitude

Other than to stand in the long silence,
the lengthening shadow, of these two

figures carved from marble—
his mother and father—

what brings him back here?
Other than to regard them

as they were before
everything went wrong. Before,

when the big globe raised between them,
so old a memory now, was still his home.

I

"Fire Destroys Beloved Chicago Bakery"

How is it that you misread "fire"
as "father"—*your* father—
come back from the dead,

to sweep, like hard wind, through the building,
to smash, with a Louisville Slugger,
every pastry with which you'd pack

your sweet little mouth, then
flick a lit match into the trash bin?
The entire building

will have to be demolished
because the father took hours
finally to be put out;

it was a stubborn father. *Your* father
who once, outside a grocery store,
warned you against asking

for anything inside, so you have learned
to keep your appetites a secret.
And how good you are: refusing,

in the drive thru, the hot apple pie
(two for a dollar), choosing
the house salad over french fries.

But maybe this is why
they all leave you, why you can't let him
rest in peace. The real question is

not why your father would do such a thing,
but why you smell him in every ruin, every
smoldering heap of ash and brick?

Landscape in Red by David Siqueiros

Whoever said that, with time, the forest
        behind the house would come back

lied—the forest still scorched
        with sorrow. If you sit in ash

long enough, its residue gets in your throat
        (odd to think you could

carry the dead forest around inside you for years)
        yet sometimes I'd go out back and sit

in what ash hadn't blown away.
        Before the fire, my father

left, angry. He went for a walk.
        That night, the forest caught fire.

Firemen said no one was to blame.
        But there's always someone.

Nighthawks by Edward Hopper

See how closely she sits to the man
in the blue suit? See how their hands
almost touch? How she reminds me
of my mother—a woman in red

drinking coffee. See?
Hopper was obviously lonely.
Why else would he paint her, my mother,
sitting there like this?

Which would make me what?
The soda jerk in white?
I'm eager enough. I want to help.
Even if it means simply waiting

to light each man's cigarette.
My mother spent
nights alone, wiping coffee mugs
clean of dust. How the lines

that creased her mouth deepened . . .
See? And what if she died
this way—sad, untouched?
I say, I want to help

but it's as if my voice is a faucet
running, a refrigerator's empty hum.
Hopper was obviously lonely.
Why else paint the gray-suited man

at the counter, my father, his back turned?

Penelope, Birdwatching

A mockingbird alights,
softly, on a branch
that seems always to brace itself, ready

in case the bird takes flight
or the bird decides to settle,
which it never does,

or not for very long,
but what can the branch do
except wait—to be pared down,

to one day snap
beneath the bird's growing weight?
And what does it say about me

who, with binoculars, watches?
(Is it wrong to watch?)
What does it mean

if sometimes I feel haunted by an absence?
Outside my apartment, the wasps
sound as if they're humming

fragments of old hymns.
Soon men with hammers
and chisels in their tool belts,

men whose jawlines are dusted
with plaster powder and sawdust,
will come and take the hive away

and I'm afraid
that I will miss the wasps
and their song, but that's foolish.

I could say my heart is heavy,
but what would that prove? Yes,
my heart is heavy. And also feels empty.

Today there's a mockingbird
on a branch, though I'm never sure
whether it's the same

mockingbird, too hard to tell.
Mostly because whenever
you see one, it's singing

a different song:
a blues.

"Love Don't Live Here Anymore"

She thought she was alone.
        My father had left her.

She'd hum in the kitchen—
        she thought she was alone—

her song the sound
        a needle makes lapping

the innermost groove of an LP,
        almost a screech—

she thought she was alone
        since dad had left her, leaving behind

some burnt down trees.
        Of course, he left

us both, but I was still there,
        watching from the kitchen door

the scar he left
        inching up her legs and arms

and all around her neck.
        (What loss doesn't scar you like that?)

When she thought *I* felt alone,
she'd sing to me.

But her screech, her screech . . .
it was deafening.

Based on a True Story

"From China the long and supple
One-winged peehees that fly in couples"
Guillaume Apollinaire, "Zone" (trans. Samuel Beckett)

I want to explain how peehees braid their necks,
but you probably won't believe me—
so instead, I'll tell you of two men

who sit across from each other
in the coffee shop, each craning the lamp
of his body over the newspaper, the crossword section,

one chewing the tip of his eraser before
passing his pencil to the other; they search for words,
these men who, for all I know, may be brothers

(that said, they could easily
mean anything or nothing to one another).
And if they are brothers,

I want to believe that when they get stuck,
one picks up his phone and dials
their father; their father who, I hope,

is a man with answers but, more than likely,
is a man trying to call back a word himself.
Who *isn't* trying to call a word

back into meaning, into use?
Like "father" for instance. Dear father. I have
multitudes of crossword puzzles. I need your help.

Power Outage Elegy

My daughter can't understand
why, when I press the button,
the parking garage door doesn't budge.

The car stuck. The park too far
for her small legs to walk. *These things
happen*, I say. *It's no one's fault.*

In the apartment courtyard, the tenants are gathered—
one complains he's missing the Laker game,
one can't charge her cell phone,

another's laptop is dead.
                              The power,
of course, isn't the problem—we're each unprepared

for such sudden loss, loss
that will last for the foreseeable future.
We're unprepared

for our little disappointments.
Normally I might not pay attention
to sunlight pouring into the courtyard

but this afternoon, I do—
probably because it's already nearly gone.
None of us mentions the night,

but I, for one, would like to
be expecting it, when
it comes.

After Word of My Uncle's Illness

Tomorrow I'll drive my mother the many miles to see him
but won't know which radio station is best for filling that frequency
of silence. Not the silence upon first hearing but, rather, Mother

mouthing a little prayer (when did she last pray?)
over her pasta—*that* silence—calling my uncle by name.
I imagine it will be much like the silence of the prophet

awaiting a word from the Lord. And then the silence of the Lord.

Gluttony

Someone told you STOP, but you still eat
and eat and eat, even eat your feet.
You eat your knees, you eat your shoes.
You eat the salmon and eat its nose.

Someone told you NO, but you still eat.
You're on a train, you're in your seat
all grown up but someone said STOP, don't eat
the girl's red bonnet, her prized red hat,

which you did anyhow. (Why listen to that?)
You're hungry for fruit, an orange, a peach.
You're hungry for dough—a pie, some bread.
Someone told you STOP, you'll soon be dead.

So what, you say. You're not my dad.

The Book of Acts

began with a group of grown men,
the disciples (whose bodies I can't help
but picture as slim as street signs), huddled

in that upper room awaiting the return of another man,
who promised to never leave them, who said he'd come back.
And they waited. Believing he would keep his word.

I spent god-knows how many days outside,
plinking nickels off a fire hydrant near the curb,
where a man, who was not my father, parked his raggedy

pick-up, and blazed by me up the apartment steps.

The Gap

Here's how it happened:
you slipped the cap gun under your t-shirt

and got caught.
The manager, merciful.

He tried your mother
who would not answer.

The police escorted you
home where a man waited.

You lost a tooth. For a long time,
you tongued that place

where the tooth used to live.
You couldn't help it.

Always looking.

Hide and Seek

Come out come out wherever you are—
The jig is up, the oxen free.
So soon the streetlamps come on like stars,
Come out come out wherever you are
Or I'll slide the latch, I'll board the door,
Not let you in—I'll eat the key.
So you, come out, whoever you are.
The jig is up, the oxen free.

On Taking Alba Back to the Pound

They'll say: *We'll find a place for him.*
They'll say: *Someone will come.*

But you already know what will be done:
someone *will* come and apply light

pressure to the dog's foreleg; a fine needle
will pass into his vein—this process

should be painless. (*It's perfectly normal
and acceptable to cry*, they'll say.)
Sleep, they'll say; it's perfectly normal to accept

that you can't keep him, but you want love
to be reason enough to try. No one wants

to live with an old loneliness, but
a body, broken enough, can surprise you

with its obedience. Like the dog, it will beg,
if you ask it to. It will stay, if you say stay.

Ukulele

What now that your father,
    who taught you neither
        to string nor play the thing,

is gone? What now? The instructions
    seem easy enough: *measure string,*
        cut with scissors, slip string in

a tuning peg, take out slack.
    The instructions think you already know
        what "headstock" and "anchor" are,

and perhaps you should.
    The instructions say "touch the body."
        Say "locate its bridge"

and you listen, feel the body
    respond, the strum vibrate
        along the contortion

made by your forearm and wrist
    as you slide your fingers
        the length of its short neck.

You don't know this
    is called progression; it takes
        a week for the nylon strings to stretch,

much longer for calluses,
      the good thick ones, big red
            grooves at the ends of your fingers,

to form. But who tells you that?
      Who tells you that they hurt?
         That you'll bleed?

II

The Short Age

I

Mid-afternoon, Luckie Park.
There's one girl preparing
to slide the long blue slide

while another scales the high rock wall.
A man, stretched between

the two at the foot of the slide, ready
to catch either's fall, looks
like an open pair of scissors.

If our father never takes us to the park,
does it mean he doesn't like us?

Sometimes we hold those strenuous
Kung-Fu stances you see on TV—
The white crane, the windmill,

the bicycle with its kickstand
dug into the sandbox—

even when no one's watching.
The sensei says you cannot break
your pose; you have to be still, even

when the scraggly little dog comes by
and pees on the tree he seems

to love best. Sometimes
he doesn't show at all, but whenever
he does, I want him; I know

full-well he'd leave piles behind,
that I'd have to pick up after him.

II

Uncluttering, she calls it.
　　It doesn't matter—broken, unbroken—
Mom sells all

　　of my father's belongings:
battery charger,
　　opened sacks of charcoal,

(who could use that?)
　　a socket wrench set.
She practically gives them away

　　at the swap meet.
On the big blue tarp, my father's armchair. . .
　　It sits there heavy

with disapproval.
　　I can almost imagine
my father's glare—*what if*

　　she sells my pistol to that man
who bought the microwave?
　　The garage, when we finish,

is little more than a shell, a hole
		like the one I stood above, once,
shoveling dirt over

		a Cobra Commander Action figure
that melted, melted because of
		sunlight and neglect.

III

Mom breaks down

and buys the self-assembly gas grill,

the bulky one, on sale at Wal-Mart

with pages left blank in the Owner's Manual

intentionally. We piece it together

leg by leg, like a model; we want to mimic the picture

on the box—a family:

father flipping burgers in his Hawaiian shirt, mother planted

under her giant umbrella, no dog, but look at the children,

mouths still wide

with a marketable joy.

IV

What do you do when,
one night, your dog disappears?

When she comes back,
her hind legs nicked, her neck

chewed? When she comes back
pregnant? When, one day,

she wakes you, yelping,
and you find that a Rottweiler

has eaten all of her puppies?
What do you do

when she refuses the leash?
When she slinks from chain-link fence

to feeding dish back to the fence,
sometimes dragging that swollen belly

of hers? What do you do
when you are shaken

by her howling? What do you do?
You bury what remains of her puppies.

V

Mid-afternoon, Luckie Park.
The city should have gotten rid of
some of this equipment by now:

what with each play area rusted-over,
held together, loosely, by rickety metal beams,
corroded bolts. The city should have

fixed some of this equipment—that swing
broken for as long as I can remember,
seat snapped off the chain.

The city should caution-tape this area off;
it can't be safe for children.
Maybe my father didn't like them,

parks. He didn't like
stepping on woodchips that littered the house.
I still love the way the woodchips nestled

inside my shoes,
in the cuffs of my jeans. It made me wonder
if there was a man in charge

of replenishing them when kids,
accidentally, brought them home.
I don't want to be that man;

I'd never notice the woodchips were missing
until too late in the evening
to replace them.

Maybe you have to be much older
to notice such things,
the things that are missing,

that you stumble upon in the dead of night
when all you want is a glass of water,
something to stop the small throbbing

that keeps you, often, from getting back to sleep.

At the End

there's a bluebird,
asleep, in the pokeweed,

and we argue still—
what's pinched in its beak—

a thread of red string, perhaps
what's left of picking apart its nest?

Though I like to think of the thread as once
woven to some larger piece of cloth,

maybe your scarf.

Love Elegy in the Chinese Garden, with Koi

Near the entrance, a patch of tall grass.
Near the tall grass, long-stemmed plants;

each bending an ear-shaped cone
to the pond's surface. If you looked closely,

you could make out silvery koi
swishing toward the clouded pond's edge

where a boy tugs at his mother's shirt for a quarter.
To buy fish feed. And watching that boy,

as he knelt down to let the koi kiss his palms,
I missed what it was to be so dumb

as those koi. I like to think they're pure,
that that's why even after the boy's palms were empty,

after he had nothing else to give, they still kissed
his hands. Because who hasn't done that—

loved so intently even after everything
has gone? Loved something that has washed

its hands of you? I like to think I'm different now,
that I'm enlightened somehow,

but who am I kidding? I know I'm like those koi,
still, with their popping mouths, that would kiss

those hands again if given the chance. So dumb.

Love Elegy with Busboy

The whole mess—
pair of chopsticks pulled apart,
tarnished pot of tea,

even my fortune
(which was no good)—
we left for the busboy to clear.

I'd probably feel more
guilty if he didn't
so beautifully sweep our soiled plates

into his plastic black tub
and the strewn rice into his palm.
The salt and pepper shakers

were set next to each other again.
A new candle was lit.
You'd never know

how reckless we'd been,
how much we'd ruined.
With the table now so spotless,

who's to say we couldn't just go
back? Who says we can't start over,
if we want?

Lines Written in the Margins of the Notebook
Found outside My Car This Morning

It said he'd need "a ladder." And "electrical clips."
        He'd need "45° brackets for superstrut,"

which meant god-knows-what, except perhaps,
        that he'd finally have all he would need
to make the repairs they all thought so necessary:

he'd leave only the wooden pegs, empty chalk
        beds where once slept a sledgehammer,

and a rusted ice pick, as he worked well
        into the evening. There is so little music
as one hunk of metal bends beneath another;

but there is enough. And he must have believed
        that this work, too, would be enough, to please her,

(isn't there always a her to please?)
        but when is she ever pleased? When
is some part of the house not in need

of attention? I know, it can't be helped; who can stop
        the wind from ripping shingles off the roof, stop

the rain from coming in, from pinging
        the deep bottoms of pots which keep you awake?
You do what you can. You build a bird house

(one thing in the shape of holding another)
      from leftover wood; you leave seed

and listen for days, as nothing
      but a small hope fills it. There is so little
music anymore, and only so much silence you can stand.

Watching the Horticulturalist

He's neither
    careful, winding
        the base of the tree

with cable, pulled taut
    enough to snap, nor
        cautious with his hammer,

bluntly striking each spike
    further and further
        into the earth—

stubborn at first, though it gives—
    the willow's limbs
        strewn everywhere.

All of this work
    so maybe the tree will remain
        planted, stay in place.

It's a marvel how,
    swinging so hard,
        he never crushes a thumb,

given how often
    I've bruised myself
        (more often than I should),

unskilled
     at steadying the nail.
          How many holes had I

left in our walls?
     I suppose it doesn't matter.
          All our pictures fell.

Some only once. But after
     that, what frame could house
          its glass, fragile as glass is?

Through My Kitchen Window

mostly, I hear a phone ringing. Not much else.
Maybe I'd stand at the window more often

if the view were nicer—a lush forest
and a little doe eating red berries from a bush.

Even if she were only there briefly, even if
she never looked at me before leaping off,

it'd be better than this. What brings me here,
usually, is some dish I left out overnight.

(This time it's a brown and withering
green salad.) But I want to be able to say

that it's hope that brings me to the window,
that I made too much salad hoping for company.

Landscape with Goats by Felix Meseck

I

It was a time of famine:
a bird we couldn't name

sat on a branch every morning
heavy with the news of spring

being gone. On the path,
we found two goats roaming,

delirious, their tongues worn
from wearing tree trunks down,

to drink the water feeding the leaves.
They must have been sick

because they began eating one another,
as though each was the other's cure.

II Reprise

I wondered how long we had
been sitting across from each other
at the kitchen table, with nothing
between us.

Aubade with a Multitude of Birds

Still dark and already
the stupid birds are at it

outside the window
how could anyone possibly

be prepared for what
clamor they make

in the oak not cooing
a cacophony so many

an ill omen of birds
seemingly trying

all at once
to speak the way

children often speak
overtop one another

as if each had the most
important thing

to say *but what
could be more important*

than this you'd ask
than our small sleep

this hour we've lost
just before the awful

light slips like a thief
through the window

and maybe this noise
is really an alarm

a red bell
in each bird's throat

announcing that
something is coming

something terrible
is coming and there's

no stopping it

III

Je vous attends by Yves Tanguy

There's someone, possibly hurt, missing.

(These planks of wood are proof.)

There's a hole somewhere.

But that's only part of the story I pieced

together from bits of shipwreck—

the impenetrable fog, the disfigured

mess, makes meaning of all this.

One black boot was washed up, its laces gone.

Somehow I know to look for the other. I stand

near the sea but can't see past the fog. Useless.

But still, I look and find, I think, something

silent, and impassable, something the map

could never have predicted.

Houdini

Who would've known you'd grow so afraid of stillness,
enclosed spaces, that you'd no longer remember a time you weren't
subtracting seconds from your life, as if each breath were held?
If you had the strength to pluck your lucky quarter

from behind your wife's ear, would you have? Would she still laugh?
A teakettle boils on the stove, its steam enough
to unlock your lungs. Your wife reads from *Robinson Crusoe*,
whom you cannot help but dream of, enveloped

by endless miles of ocean. Outside, paper skeletons are strung
up on every house in your neighborhood. You hear a boy
skipping up and down the block, begging his mother,
for Halloween, *Mom, can I please be a ghost, please?*

Altar Call

Our Father, which
>> art in
>>>> organs, kneelers overlaid

with silk or velvet,
>> reupholstered pews.
>>>> Our Father,

which art
>> in the brilliant past tense,
>>>> when priests slid back

the paneling, pressed
>> lips to window screens
>>>> and whispered *Tell me*

sins. My mother
>> led me to the altar
>>>> where I knelt,

hands clasped between
>> my thighs. The congregation hummed
>>>> "Just As I Am,"

a wafer softened
>> on my tongue. The pastor touched
>>>> them, woman after woman. Touched, my mother

collapsed.
        (Was it the hand of God?)
           I waited for

one to come and lay
        her hands on me,
           soak her fingertips in oil,

anoint my forehead
        with a kiss. Near me were women
           who lugged clay jugs from Egypt

in their chests, who flooded
        the altar with songs.
           Near me were women

who writhed like fish
        on shag,
           skirts silvery and hiked.

The church bells clanged.
        In the parking lot, I
           witnessed the pastor light

a cigarette.
        But who would believe
           me? Once

I even saw an angel, pomegranate seeds
cupped in her hands.
                       Take, she bade me. *Eat.*

Love Elegy outside Eden

My dearest rib, if
  with the ear

nested in the center
  of the heart, you list-

en, somewhere within me, too,
  a city is blank-

eted in flakes of ash,
  and a flock of geese

cleave the winter
  with a scalpel's

ease. The geese
  honk overhead

where
  art thou? And I answer,

"Here, in the garden,
  where nothing lives."

I am not thinking, only
  wavering too long above

this pond, which offers
  mud and dead fish

as reflection. I forget who left me
        this heavy

fist, and this blue bucket,
        all this ice and salt.

Love Elegy with Imaginary Fire

It's how Nancy teaches her daughter
to be more punctual—*Pretend you're on fire!*
Her point is that you can

save yourself. It's easy. Her daughter doesn't
get it, why sweat such a small thing,
an alarm you forgot to set—who cares?

Who hasn't been guilty of that? But then—
The cat's dead! C'mon!
Her point is that anything can be saved

if you reach it in time. I'll admit,
I've never thought to try this method.
You see, Nancy's daughter

is the same age as mine.
(Guinea pig's dead!)
It's been a year now, since

I've seen her. Nancy says nothing
about neglect. How it too, at first, seems
so small a thing. And who

hasn't done it? She *does* say that
her daughter, after lacing snow boots
slowly, saunters across the room

and strokes the cat into purring.
Blows tiny kisses into the guinea pig's cage.
The nerve, right?

Her daughter doesn't get it.
They're already gone.
I don't know what amount

of tenderness could change that.

On the City Bus

The boy wants to pull the cord, because he's learned
that the bus, as large as it is, will listen, but
his father won't allow it. They head towards wherever
they were already headed. And watching, I've missed
my stop. . . . Wasn't this among the lessons I was taught

as my mother pressed quarters into my palm
and sent me off alone? "Boy, pay attention
to the driver. Pay attention to where you are.
Know how far this line will take you.
Know when it's time to pull the cord."

Odysseus, Delayed

You stand in front of the airport window, watching
the planes arrive, or leave. Or you watch the sky, dark now,
smog where—weren't there stars here before? Wait long enough

and you'll find yourself alone with this evening—though beautiful
women pass with their sons, boys like your own who you may never
see again. Listen. A name's called again, over the intercom.

He has kept everyone waiting, whoever he is—still not responding.

Love Elegy with Tea House

I don't have to tell you how this ends.
He stood under the cherry blossom tree
and then, moving closer, I saw him

inside the tea house, handling a ceramic—always
the breakable objects. He had to have slipped
under the tape (the tea house bordered

by yellow tape). Deceitful. Did I blame him
for following me (*Yes, yes, I did.*)—for the ravage
he left behind?—The ginkgos already stripped

and suddenly, I was so thirsty I fluttered above
the honeysuckle bush though I could not sip.

Scale

At the Griffith Observatory,
which you mostly like to visit

alone, there is a seismograph,
and beneath it a plaque that reads:

"When two plates grind
against each other, tensions

build. Eventually, something
has to give." You jump

on the seismograph; its
needle, which has scratched

in red the weight of everyone
who's come before you, doesn't

register your weight. There is no one
to tell you it's broken;

you'd always wished it to be broken.
If this Earth is your home,

if it's crumbling under you,
how saddening to know

how little you matter.
Not that this is news.

Late-hour Poem, with My Daughter a Town Away

The twin comforter, thick and heavily starched,
must be why you cannot sleep, this bed
not yours.

               In the air, a rat perhaps,
dead in one of the vents, you wonder. Alone?
You cannot sleep. The ceiling stain.

Nothing on television, but the blue light
bathing the wall is pleasant, cool. The Front Desk
tells you to report any cockroaches, a reminder

that things are
               shifting, unseen, all around you.

Used Camaro

It's your daughter's birthday; she's expecting
you, and you're late: flat tire.
You're waiting for the tow to arrive

when you remember the mechanic
who, changing the oil, advised
that you tag and scrap the old girl.

That's what he called your Camaro:
The old girl. He said she had salvageable parts,
but wouldn't hold up forever

(though what does) and so you've taken
the old girl as far as she will go.
This time that means learning

to work the lug wrench and car jack yourself.
(Who else is there to teach you?)
That means feeling along the shoulder

of an unfamiliar road with a flashlight.
You want to be angry—
with the tow truck driver, with the old girl—

for how long you've been waiting,
but think of your daughter—
isn't she waiting, too? (Not to worry, though,

it's not as if you haven't
failed her before.) The balloons
in the back seat are sinking. The cake

crumbling. Even if you make it,
jeans oil-smudged and streaked,
you hate to let her see you like this.

To Have Light

Somewhere on I-5, in the flash of hazard lights,
I was broken-down. But it seemed enough to have light.

The piano playing itself in the hall needs
tuning, its notes ghostly and bent in the half-light.

Tennis shoes and tin cans tied to the car the couple
rushed out toward, struck by rice and the sun's grave light.

Before sorrow was the garden, the man and woman,
the tree—forbidden. Before sorrow, God gave light.

Orpheus repeats his great sin of looking back. . . .
Is it memory—*regret*—calling from the cave's poor light?

She walked with the brilliance of a sequined dress. How
could I ignore such shimmer, such provocative light?

Then, the birds attended her: seagulls circled and wailed.
And on the telephone line, the mourning doves alighted.

"When the one they were expecting came into the room. . ." Then,
there—Nathan, a flame in their eyes: they were slaves to his light.

Consolation

Let's say, waiting to board the plane,
you noticed a woman on her cell phone.

Of course, she was beautiful,
but what made you notice

was that you could tell, by her gestures,
that her phone call was bad—

how first she ducked away
from who could've been her sister, cupped

her hand over her mouth. How she wept so openly.

And you wanted to say something
(certainly you have some wisdom for this)

but what do you say? *"Whatever it is, I'm sorry"*?
"There is always something

to be made of pain"?
I said nothing. Because sometimes

language has already done enough;
if you don't believe me, try

explaining absence to my eight-year-old girl.
Try imagining how large her silence has grown.

70

What do you say? I said nothing.

When we were boarding the plane,
as others fished through their carry-ons

for tissue, nothing. I thought, soon
we'll be past all this. You'll feel lighter.

This is what I tell myself.

The Sculpture

because there was a black girl there they said
in the garden by the river and I looked because

follow the geese they said their broken formation
they said follow the river and there she was

made to sit pulled to herself her forearms crossed
because she laid her head against them

as if she were asleep *honey are you asleep*
because she was silent on a stone slab

or her silence was that of a black girl
who had swallowed a large stone

because I had no blanket
and snow clumped on her shoulders

because someone left her like that *where did he go*
because she might have looked up because I looked

by the river it kept whispering *hush* and the stone was
quiet and the black girl so quiet because I was

going out of the garden with the loud geese *you have to*
tell her they said because

the frozen sheet of river also splits
because the black girl was still mine I called her

Night they said *was she made to sit like this*
or *if you could give sadness a shape*

or *until it hardens you have to leave it alone*
because they nodded yes and yes

and the black girl was quiet
she laid her head against them

because wasn't she a sweet black girl
she did everything she was told

Manantiales

How could I not, look back now, remember—
the sign that read *No Dogs Allowed*

In The Water even as one man wrestled his
into the stream, which was shallow

yet already full of girls slapping a volleyball
back and forth or flinging their arms

around the boys. The things boys will do
for a girl—send a tennis shoe bobbing like a great ship

over the small waves. What a beautiful thing
to watch—and watch I did,
pulling apart the carpels of an orange

from a safe distance, watched those boys,
little cannonballs, throwing themselves

from the high boulder, spitting water,
giggling at each other—such youth

and recklessness. Watched, after you
dove into the stream fully clothed,

you sit upon a gray stone, hair almost glistening,
knees pulled up beneath your chin.

"A Guided Tour of the Kykuit Sculpture Garden"

might be a bit of a stretch. They must've meant:
brochure in hand, you get to
walk this quiet garden on your own.

Or: we trust this map
should help you figure out
what it is you're looking at

("*Orpheus* maybe?
*Woman and Bird? Hercules
and the Hydra?*")

Who knows? Perhaps,
if I'd run across the man
responsible for waxing each

limestone shoulder, every
copper throat, the slope
of each polished bronze thigh

with a small tin and a dry white cloth,
I could be certain.
Then again, what would he care?

*You try doing this year after year.
See if you don't get tired of beauty.*
Who doesn't at times tire of beauty?

Who doesn't tire of grief?
Who doesn't tire
of, again, writing the poem

in which one must track,
through a sheet of clean snow,
the fox

(or whatever)
that's vanished?
In which one calls each shape

the trees rehearse
behind a curtain of fog
ruin, or *longing*,

or some other undoing.
My guide, were I
provided with a guide,

might likely say
I should be less dramatic.
Then he might gesture toward

the black sculpture up ahead—*"Dans La Nuit . . ."*
Let me paint the picture for you:
two bronze figures recline,

naked, in the grass. Snow
is piled all around them. Even now,
it's almost impossible to tell

the two apart—her head fixed
to his chest, how their legs
have so entwined. . . .

What more is there to say, really?
Other than the long history
of these two figures finally at rest,

the piece needs no decoration
but this wind. Love,
may our life together be that simple.

Lie here with me.
Let me say your name.
Let that be plenty.

Acknowledgments

My gratitude goes to the editors of the following journals, in which the poems in this book, sometimes in earlier versions, first appeared: *The Collagist*, *Connotation Press: An Online Artifact*, *District Lit*, *Inch*, *Iron Horse Literary Review*, *The Journal*, *Muzzle Magazine*, *New Haven Review*, *The Oneiric Moor*, *Ploughshares*, *Quarterly West*, *SalonZine*, *Southern Humanities Review*, *Southern Indiana Review*, *Sou'wester*, *Toe Good Poetry*, *Union Station Magazine*, *Waxwing*, and *Weave Magazine*.

"*Landscape with Goats* by Felix Meseck" appears in the anthology *Best New Poets 2010*, selected by Claudia Emerson.

"*Landscape with Goats* by Felix Meseck" was reprinted in *phatitude Literary Magazine: Spring Has Returned: A Season of Renewal* (March 2, 2011).

"'Fire Destroys Beloved Chicago Bakery'" is for Ivone Alexandre. "*Manantiales*" is for Laura Swearingen-Steadwell. "A Guided Tour of the Kykuit Sculpture Garden" is for Carrie Addington.

There are far too many individuals to thank for their encouragement, endless support, and insight during the making of this book. A tremendous thank you to Ivone Alexandre (for far more than I can list), Claire Hellar, Ross White, Jonathan Callies, Francine Conley, Carrie Mar, Tommye Blount (my dear, dear brother), Sean Patrick Hill, Ladan Osman (I truly adore you), Jennifer Büchi, Phillip B. Williams, Laura Swearingen-Steadwell (many thank yous), Lynne Procope, Reed Wilson, Chris Abani, Patricia Smith, Matthew Olzmann, Vievee Francis, Tom Sleigh, Ama Codjoe, Dena Gast, Maura Conley, Denise Clary, Rebecca Lund, Stephen Yenser, and Carrie Addington (for being my reader, and so much more—thank you, thank you; one poem doesn't nearly suffice). I'm sorry, I'm sure I've left out names. . . .

To Ellen Bryant Voigt, Debra Allbery, C. Dale Young, Stephen Dobyns, Jennifer Grotz, Martha Rhodes, Joan Aleshire, and my great friends and peers at the MFA Program for Writers at Warren Wilson: thank you for making my graduate experience nothing short of magic.

Immense gratitude for their generous financial support, fellowship, and precious gifts of time, to Maudelle Driskell, Patrick Donnelly, and Martha Rhodes of The Frost Place; Michael Collier and Jennifer Grotz of the Bread Loaf Writers' Conference; Toi Derricotte, Cornelius Eady, and Allison Myers of Cave Canem; Susanne Pandich, The Rockefeller Brothers Fund, and the Pocantico Conference Center and staff for the Pocantico Residency at the Marcel Breuer House in Tarrytown, New York.

Special thanks to my family for supporting me, especially when you didn't understand. To Greg Gilbert and Steve Mueske, for starting all this. To Jillian Rowen, for continually supporting me and, more importantly, my work, with your all, and always ensuring I am surrounded by the art of others. Thank you, endlessly, for you. But mostly, for love and stuff.

Finally, boundless thanks to Martha Rhodes for believing in this book. Thank you to my editor, Ryan Murphy, and the entire staff of Four Way Books for making me family. This book is one I wanted— *needed*—to write. Thank you.

Nathan McClain is a Southern California native. He's received scholarships from the Bread Loaf Writers' Conference and The Frost Place. His poems have appeared or are forthcoming in *Iron Horse Literary Review*, *Ploughshares*, *Quarterly West*, *Southern Indiana Review*, and *Sou'wester*, among others. Nathan is a graduate of the MFA Program for Writers at Warren Wilson, as well as a Cave Canem fellow. He currently lives in Brooklyn and teaches writing at the College of Staten Island and Drew University.

Publication of this book was made possible by grants and donations. We are also grateful to those individuals who participated in our 2016 Build a Book Program. They are:

Anonymous (8), Evan Archer, Sally Ball, Jan Bender-Zanoni, Zeke Berman, Kristina Bicher, Carol Blum, Lee Briccetti, Deirdre Brill, Anthony Cappo, Carla & Steven Carlson, Maxwell Dana, Machi Davis, Monica Ferrell, Martha Webster & Robert Fuentes, Dorothy Goldman, Lauri Grossman, Steven Haas, Mary Heilner, Henry Israeli, Christopher Kempf, David Lee, Jen Levitt, Howard Levy, Owen Lewis, Paul Lisicky, Katie Longofono, Cynthia Lowen, Louise Mathias, Nathan McClain, Gregory McDonald, Britt Melewski, Kamilah Moon, Carolyn Murdoch, Tracey Orick, Zachary Pace, Gregory Pardlo, Allyson Paty, Marcia & Chris Pelletiere, Eileen Pollack, Barbara Preminger, Kevin Prufer, Peter & Jill Schireson, Roni & Richard Schotter, Soraya Shalforoosh, Peggy Shinner, James Snyder & Krista Fragos, Megan Staffel, Marjorie & Lew Tesser, Susan Walton, Calvin Wei, Abigail Wender, Allison Benis White, and Monica Youn.